20 LESSONS

THAT

BUILD A MAN'S
FRIENDS

20 LESSONS
THAT
BUILD A MAN'S FRIENDS

A CONVERSATIONAL MENTORING GUIDE

VINCE MILLER

EQUIP PRESS

Colorado Springs

20 LESSONS
THAT
BUILD A MAN'S
FRIENDS

Published by Equip Press, Colorado Springs, CO

Scripture quotations marked (ESV) are taken from The ESV® Bible (The Holy Bible, English Standard Version®) copyright © 2001 by Crossway, a publishing ministry of Good News Publishers. ESV® Text Edition: 2011. The ESV® text has been reproduced in cooperation with and by permission of Good News Publishers. Unauthorized reproduction of this publication is prohibited. Used by permission. All rights reserved.

Scripture quotations marked (KJV) are taken from the King James Bible. Accessed on Bible Gateway at www.BibleGateway.com.

Scripture quotations marked (NASB) are taken from the New American Standard Bible® (NASB), copyright © 1960, 1962, 1963, 1968, 1971, 1972, 1973, 1975, 1977, 1995 by The Lockman Foundation, www.Lockman.org. Used by permission.

Scripture quotations marked (NIV) are taken from the Holy Bible, New International Version. Copyright © 1973, 1978, 1984, 2011 by Biblica, Inc.® Used by permission. All rights reserved worldwide.

Scripture quotations marked (NKJV) are taken from the New King James Version®. Copyright © 1982 by Thomas Nelson, Inc. Used by permission. All rights reserved.

Scripture quotations marked (NLT) are taken from the Holy Bible, New Living Translation, copyright © 1996, 2004, 2015 by Tyndale House Foundation. Used by permission of Tyndale House Publishers, Inc., Carol Stream, Illinois 60188. All rights reserved.

Scripture quotations marked (NRSV) are taken from the New Revised Standard Version Bible, copyright © 1989 the Division of Christian Education of the National Council of the Churches of Christ in the United States of America. Used by permission. All rights reserved.

First Edition: 2020
20 Lessons That Build A Man's Friends / Vince Miller
Paperback ISBN: 978-1-951304-21-8
eBook ISBN: 978-1-951304-22-5

EQUIP PRESS

Colorado Springs

TO: _____

FROM: _____

NOTE: _____

_____

_____

_____

_____

_____

_____

_____

_____

_____

_____

_____

_____

_____

_____

_____

CONTENTS

A Note From The Author   9

How To Use Twenty Lessons That Build a Man's Friends   11

Speaker & Author Vince Miller   13

1. Signs of a Great Friend   15
2. The Importance of Brotherhood   19
3. How to Find Wise Counsel?   23
4. Giving Attention   27
5. Life After the Shenanigans   33
6. Nathan & David   37
7. Moses & Aaron   43
8. Paul & Barnabas   47
9. Shadrach, Meshach, & Abednego   53
10. David & Jonathan   57
11. Paul & Timothy   63
12. Moses & Jethro   69
13. Beyond Perceptions   75
14. Build Emotional Disclosure   81
15. 6 Reasons Why Guys Need Guy Friends   85
16. Man Is Not Meant to Do Life Alone   91
17. Isolation Is Our Enemy   95
18. Forging Friendships   99
19. Are We Afraid of Bromance   103
20. Reconciling Friendships   107

A NOTE FROM THE AUTHOR

Friendships are important to men. Yet many men fail to take initiative when it comes to relationships with Christian brothers. We may just be afraid of the bromance. But we shouldn't. Male friendships in Christ are necessary for shaping us as men.

My hope for you is that these lessons give you something to discuss with a friend, relative, coworker, or even your children. I hope they will stir a discussion that will give you an opportunity to be proactive in your friendships, and to pass on wisdom. May this mentoring relationship guide lead to greater success as you lead your business, team, non-profit, church, or your own family.

Let me encourage you to become part of a mentorship movement, either to mentor or be mentored.

Keep moving forward,

Live all in,

HOW TO USE TWENTY LESSONS THAT BUILD A MAN'S FRIENDS

The Purpose

This 20-lesson guide is for mentors to use in private reflection or conversations with others. It's written to encourage conversations about leadership and character development among people of any age. It can be used repeatedly.

The Process

First, build yourself

Each time you read through a lesson, ponder privately on the reflection questions within the lesson. These lessons use the B.U.I.L.D. process:

- BEGIN with the goal.
- UNPACK your thoughts.
- INFORM through the Bible.
- LAND on action steps.
- DO one action for one week.

Second, partner up

Take each lesson further by partnering up with someone else. Use the 20 lessons as a mentoring tool that takes all the guesswork out of a leadership development conversation. Partner up with a friend, relative, co-worker, or someone in your family.

The Payoff

If you stay with the process for all 20 lessons you will grow in character, in your leadership, and in community with others. Often, we just need a plan to get moving. This book provides that plan—a method and a process that results in outcomes with a rich payoff.

SPEAKER & AUTHOR VINCE MILLER

Abandoned at the age of two by his drug-using father, Vince Miller grew up in a challenging and anxiety-producing environment. He endured the strain of his mother's two failed marriages as well as her own drug use and poor choices. Fortunately, during Vince's formative teen years his grandfather, a man of faith, stepped up to mentor Vince, guiding him through a particularly difficult period.

Though he resisted initially, at the age of 20 Vince became a follower of Christ. Soon after, he would be at his grandfather's deathbed when cancer took his life. At that time Vince committed before God to "give back" by mentoring men as his grandfather had mentored him. Vince's story demonstrates the importance of mentors to support others in overcoming the enormous hurdles that manhood, mentoring, fathering, and leadership present to a man who wants to live in faith and character.

Audiences respond to Vince's stories. His teaching motivates, convicts, and sometimes even shock the listener. He inspires men to lead and mentor others with an intelligent argument for faith and stories of choices he made as a man, husband, father, and leader.

After serving in notable organizations for over 26 years (including Young Life, InterVarsity, and TCU Football), Vince founded *Resolute*, a non-profit organization focused on providing men with tools for mentorship. He's written 16 books and Bible study handbooks, along with producing small group videos that are resources for mentorship. His website, vincemiller. com, contains a Men's Daily Devotional read by thousands daily.

If you are looking for a motivational and engaging communicator for your next retreat, conference, or event, you can reach out to Vince Miller directly: www.vincemiller.com

Signs of a Great Friend

"A man of many companions may come to ruin, but there is a friend who sticks closer than a brother."

(PROVERBS 18:24)

True lifelong friends are hard to find, mostly because over time people change, as do we. But when shared values, shared life experiences, and shared seasons meet, we look over and discover there is a friend waiting with whom we can often link arms.

This is one of the great perks of being a Christian. We don't have to question (at least too much) the shared value we have in God and his Scripture. And this takes a lot of the mystery out of brotherhood. Yet we still have the obstacles of everyday life that prohibit friendship. Even so, there are friends that will stick with us through these changing seasons. There are those who will stick closer than a brother, simply because they care. And they frequently show they care in these ways.

One | They care about our relationship with God first.

But seek first the kingdom of God and his righteousness,
and all these things will be added to you.

(Matthew 6:33)

True friends have one spiritual priority, both for themselves and for us: God and his righteous way of life. Everything else is a radical second. While we may talk about politics, sports, and the latest issue at work, they have a mind for God. They care about how we think, how we discuss, how we respond, and even more, our *attitude* regarding all these things. They are concerned with matters of the heart and how to consistently keep our heart, character, and spirit aligned with God's will.

Two | They love unconditionally, but also want us to change.

A friend loves at all times, and a brother is born for adversity.

(Proverbs 17:17)

Without a doubt we need to be loved. Men don't like to use this term but that is exactly what it is: love. Many times, this love will exceed that of a flesh and blood brother because it is less presumptive and more gracious. This is unconditional love with no strings attached. But this does not mean it accepts disobedience without a desire for change, for this would actually be *un*loving. We need brothers that lovingly accept us but also want a better future for us; and this demands change. This is true brotherly love.

Three | They rush to our aid when we need it.

And behold, some men were bringing on a bed a man who was paralyzed, and they were seeking to bring him in and lay him before Jesus, but finding no way to bring him in, because of the crowd, they went up on the roof and let him down with his bed through the tiles into the midst before Jesus.

(Luke 5:18-19)

Yep, this is pretty cool. This man had some friends and they all wanted the best for him. Their friendship was so strong they went overboard for him. They pushed through the crowds, dug through a roof, and lowered him carefully and strategically at the feet of Jesus. How about that for friendship?

I have read this story many times and asked myself, "Do I have friends like that?" Friends that will come to my aid at fourth-and-goal, even when it puts them out? We should all ask ourselves this question.

But there may be a far more important question to ask ourselves. Are *you* that type of friend? Are you a friend that cares about your brother's relationship with God? Do you unconditionally love but want to see your brother change? Do you rush to your brother's aid? If not, then be a friend today! You may discover along the road of life that simply by being a great friend, you will make great friends.

Just hear these words from our greatest friend, the friend of sinners: Jesus Christ.

Greater love has no one than this:
that someone lay down his life for his friends.

(John 15:13)

Reflection & Mentorship

Begin

- There are signs of a great friend and brother, so be that brother.

Unpack

- Have you ever been burned by a friend?

- Listed above are three signs of great friends: can you think of other signs?
- Why do men never talk about stuff like this, especially friendships with other men?

Inform

- Which of the three points above did you need to be reminded about today?
- Which one do you need to act on?

Land

- What action do you need to take?

Do

- Be a better friend and pray for better friendships.

The Importance of Brotherhood

"For where two or three are gathered in my name,
there am I among them."

(MATTHEW 18:20)

Brothers, I'm just going to say it: *we need each other.* But our culture would have us believe otherwise, wouldn't it? Our culture encourages a solitary, independent, "I can do this alone" attitude among men. We're told, "Real men don't need anyone else," and we've taken the bait, hook, line, and sinker. And as a result most guys do not have a close male friend. How can this be good?

It's not. As is often the case, truth flies in the face of culture. Real men know they need each other. While autonomy may come easily for us, we've got to live out our quest for manhood in the context of brotherhood with other believers. Within Christian brotherhood that we discover the riches of the deep spiritual relationship modeled to us by the Godhead: Father, Son, and Holy Spirit. It is also through brotherhood that we live out faith, love, and oneness that extends God's message of grace and reconciliation to the world. This is the environment where iron sharpens iron, and we voluntarily put ourselves in proximity with other men to avoid the catastrophes in our lives that would unravel our manhood.

So how do we achieve the "iron sharpens iron" synergy that promotes true Christian brotherhood? Here are three strategies to get us started.

One | Transparency

Search me, O God, and know my heart! Try me and know my thoughts! And see if there be any grievous way in me, and lead me in the way everlasting!

(Psalm 139:23-24)

In this text, David is transparent, open, honest, and vulnerable with God. This is where great men are made, right here in utter honesty with God. But transparency also transfers into other relationships as well. As it should. Because a fearless man like David was not afraid of facing the enemy of pride. He knew that pride tempts us to put on a front for others when—on the inside—we are falling apart.

We should get real about the issues and challenges we face. Knowing who we are in Christ and embracing the forgiveness that is ours because of what He did on the cross, let's move beyond the fear and shame that cause us to pretend, and instead live in full self-disclosure and freedom from the bondage of sin.

Two | Accountability

So then each of us will give an account of himself to God.

(Romans 14:12)

God is all about accountability, from the first pages of the Bible to the last. And we might as well embrace it; because based on what we read here, we will not escape it. So why not learn accountability now, so when it happens we will not be surprised?

Let's willingly submit ourselves to accountability with other brothers, not just the loving but convicting "no, don't do that" brand of accountability, but also the encouraging accountability that says, "I am behind you; let's do this together."

Three | Consistency

Therefore, my beloved brothers, be steadfast, immovable, always abounding in the work of the Lord, knowing that in the Lord your labor is not in vain.

(1 Corinthian 15:58)

Let's be intentional about getting together. Rarely will it happen just by accident. You might even set a standing date to meet with a brother, like the first and third Thursday of every month, for example. Make it count. Build relationships that go beyond the casual, relationships that drive us to deeper levels of awareness of each other and the challenges we face.

"And let us consider how to stir up one another to love and good works, not neglecting to meet together, as is the habit of some, but encouraging one another..."

(Hebrews 10:24-25)

Jesus was a radical. He was not one to acquiesce to errant cultural trends. By his teaching and by his example, we see that true Christian brotherhood is essential to our spiritual health. It's got to be a priority. Paul challenges us in Romans 12:10, "Love one another with brotherly affection. Outdo one another in showing honor."

Let's get radical. Let's do this.

Reflection & Mentorship

Begin

- Brotherhood is important and we need a strategy for building it.

Unpack

- What strategy do men typically use for building brotherhood? Or do they have one?
- Why do we not have a strategy? Are we lazy, busy, or is there another reason?

Inform

- Which of these three points above is hard for you?
- Why is this so, and what issues might you need to address?

Land

- How do you need to adapt your strategy today?
- What steps do you need to take?

Do

- Reach out to a friend using your new strategy.

How to Find Wise Counsel?

The more man knows of man, the better
for the common brotherhood among men."

CHARLES DICKENS

Sometimes we don't know exactly how to approach a new relationship with another man, or even how to broach the topic of counsel. Sometimes we are overly concerned that is will make us look stupid, incompetent, ignorant, or the like. But living in this place of personal shame prevents us from getting the counsel we need.

Taking the first step is the hardest. After this we build the competence and awareness that it is relationships with other Godly men that make us better. We discover that God has invented the best pro-bono system for getting everything we need and that Christian brothers are required to help. It's our Christian duty. And who isn't endeared when another man asks for wisdom? I love it when men ask men a question I can easily answer; it makes me feel appreciated.

So here are some suggestions for men seeking counsel and growth in wisdom in their life.

One | Seek counsel from older men.

Find a godly man about ten years your senior and draw wisdom from him. By listening to an older, wiser, more mature man who has "been around the block a few times," you will discover nuances in decision-making that will help you as you make decisions. They are voices who possess deep spiritual insight and who are known to seek God's direction for themselves.

Two | Seek counsel from men who have faced your issues.

Talk not only to those who have plenty of life experience but also to those who perhaps have faced decisions similar to yours in the past. Buy them a meal, and spend a little time learning from how they handled their challenges. Discover the issues and problems they faced and what they learned through the process.

Three | Seek counsel from men who challenge you.

While it's easy to seek counsel only from those who you know ahead of time will agree with what you think, maybe you need to hear from those who have a contrarian voice. And when I say contrarian, I mean contrarian in their delivery as well as their point of view. Every one of us knows a person with a ton of life wisdom whose personality, approach, and opinions challenge us. And while we don't like to invite them to speak into our life, they often have knowledge that we can discover. Even disagreeable people have learned great truths throughout their life. Finding *"the meat and tossing the bones"* is part of our job in seeking the truth, even from disagreeable people. Wise people learn how to gain wisdom from people on the other side of the aisle. And men who carefully listen even to a challenging voice grow wiser just in the activity of listening.

Four | Seek counsel from men who have failed.

Men who have failed, which means all of us, fail for specific reasons. They have learned insightful lessons, and you need to learn from them. They are often waiting to tell you how to avoid the same mistakes. You will even get to hear and perhaps see the ramifications from these poor choices firsthand.

Go to these men and learn from them, and do not make the same mistakes they did, but learn from what got them into their situations. This type of counsel is frequently avoided but is an excellent source of wisdom.

Five | Ask God for counsel.

> *"Trust in the Lord with all your heart, and do not lean on your own understanding. In all your ways acknowledge Him, and He will make straight your paths."*

(Proverbs 3:5-6)

Let's just put it out there: real men admit that they don't know everything. In his book *Decision Making & the Will of God,* Garry Friesen points out that the right attitude for acquiring wisdom includes humility and teachability, along with reverence, diligence, uprightness, and faith. In a nutshell, Friesen's approach to making the best decisions includes:

1. Asking God for wisdom.
2. Scouring the pages of Scripture.
3. Conducting some personal research.
4. Seeking wise counsel.
5. Looking back on (and learning from) your own life experience.

The ultimate source of wise counsel, of course, is God himself. And let's face it: even in our earnestness to make the best, most sensible, most God-honoring choices, we'll still occasionally blow it. But God is always with us. He has the power not only to use our mistakes for good but also to redirect us to the right path. Keep moving forward, confident that as you grow in spiritual maturity, you'll also get better and better at making the best choices—in part because you have chosen your counselors well.

Reflection & Mentorship

Begin

- We need to learn to seek and draw wise counsel from great people.

Unpack

- Do you think it is easy or hard to find wise counsel and counselors?
- Have you ever received bad advice from someone? What was the outcome?

Inform

- The proverb says, *"Without counsel plans fail, but with many advisers they succeed."* How is this true?
- Do you consistently seek out *"many"* advisers or counselors?
- Of the five points above, which is easy, and which is hard for you? Why?

Land

- What do you need to do differently?

Do

- Identify a list of 1-3 wise men you can turn to in life.
- Ask one of them for advice this next week.
- Report back your finding to a friend, relative, or mentor.

Giving Attention

"Just remaining quietly in the presence of God, listening to Him, being attentive to Him, requires a lot of courage and know-how."

THOMAS MERTON

"My son, be attentive to my words; incline your ear to my sayings."

(PROVERBS 4:20)

Something demands our attention:

Despite the pain they cause, we all fall into unhealthy patterns, relationships, and habits that catch up with us in the end. What we often fail to realize is that engaging in these behaviors even a few times can result in life patterns, healthy or unhealthy, that can impact our lives and the lives of those around us. Sometimes they become so habitual we're not even aware of them. And then one day we look up, and we are shocked to the see the toll these toxic patterns have taken on our physical fitness, personal relationships, and spiritual lives. Our aim should be to identify healthy life patterns that provide others and us with life, joy, and purpose, not toxic results.

One | Be fully engaged.

Now for a moment, picture a group of men lounging around. What is in the hand of almost everyone you know? A device of some kind. They are texting, emailing, surfing, and generally entertained and distracted by an onslaught of media and communication. Ironically, it is possible today to be connected superficially to more people than ever while never developing deep and meaningful friendships because we are not genuinely present to those within reach. Relationships, by definition, require presence, and presence, by its meaning, demands freedom from distractions.

Consider all the positive messages you intentionally communicate to others by giving them your full and undivided attention. By doing this, you deliberately state, without words, that you care about what they are saying. You imply you care about the relationship because you are giving all of yourself to all of them. You demonstrate that at this moment not only what they say, but also who they are, is valuable to you. These are actions of engagement and interest rather than of distraction and non-interest. I call this the "100% Rule." And the goal is to give each person you encounter 100% of you at the moment. Your wife. Your children. Your waiter. Your flight attendant. Your friend. Each human interruption and encounter, if ordained by God, requires you to give full expectation and 100% of your attention. Could you imagine Jesus sitting with his disciples, while the twelve sat around surfing the Internet on their mobile devices? Probably not, primarily because it was Jesus, and he was interesting and valuable to them. Those who develop healthy patterns of engagement with others form a powerful and needed skill in today's distracted and entertained world.

Two | Have great conversations.

The flip side of healthy engagement is learning to speak well, so that our communication is welcoming, encouraging, and a blessing to others. One healthy behavior in conversation is to remember that people are interesting.

The fastest way to get a great discussion going is to inquire *of* those and *about* those whom we interact. People love to talk about themselves, and since this is the case you should ask them questions about themselves. Great questions provoke good conversations and can quickly infiltrate surface conversations. But it requires you to stop talking about yourself.

Jesus did this all the time. He constantly asked questions. In fact, he asked questions of people who asked *him* questions. This places the questioner in a position of power. Just read this interaction and watch what Jesus does with the power of questions. He disarms a manipulative man with simple questions and drives after his heart to manipulate the moment.

> *And behold, a lawyer stood up to put him to the test, saying,*
> *"Teacher, what shall I do to inherit eternal life?" He said to him,*
> *"What is written in the Law? How do you read it?" And he*
> *answered, "You shall love the Lord your God with all your heart*
> *and with all your soul and with all your strength and with all your*
> *mind, and your neighbor as yourself." And he said to him, "You have*
> *answered correctly; do this, and you will live."*

(Luke 10:25-28)

The purpose of good conversation is to genuinely get to know another individual, to encourage them, and to mutually grow closer. Most men do not have these types of conversations since we default to transactional conversations rather than more meaningful communication. We prefer surface-level discussions about the latest sports score, political happening, business scandal, or fake news. And while there is nothing wrong with a little political sparring on current happenings, if the conversation is only a debate on issues but does not include our feelings, beliefs, attitudes, and responses to life then we will miss the opportunity for a more profound conversation. So many of our discussions today leave others no better off than when they began. Meanwhile, most of us long for a better and more in-depth conversation and relationship with others, conversations that produce thoughtful interactions, challenge, and even change in others and ourselves. We long to be understood by others and have them understand us. We long to have people with whom we can be candid and honest. We want to share our lives and journeys and have a meaningful impact.

A life skill to develop is the ability to guide conversations that help us get below the surface of life. Asking great question or making insightful observations are how to achieve this goal. When heading into a lunch, social time, or situation where you will be with others, consider what kinds of questions you might want to ask to stimulate a great conversation. Even a short preparation time will result in incredible results. It's a life-hack that will serve you well throughout your life.

Three | Get to know wise men.

How many wise men do you know personally? Hopefully you have a few, but most of us don't have any real relationships with wise men. But we can make up for this if we develop the life habit of *reading* quality material from wise men. Remember, reading is a means of getting to know sagacious people intimately. A good book is like the experience of sitting in the presence of a wise man or woman and entering into a dialogue with them on relevant topics. The higher the quality of the writing, and the more it's tied to the scripture, the higher the quality of the wisdom it produces. Authors who write this way feed, challenge, and help us think more deeply than we would otherwise. I think of men like Richard Foster, Dallas Willard, A.W. Tozer, and Charles Spurgeon who have spoken remarkable truths to me over the years and effectively mentored me in ways I will never forget.

As you read these authors, take notes on the writings of these men. Underline things that cause you to think, write your observations and thoughts in the margins. Have a dialogue with the author on those pages, or with another man, who hopefully challenges you on the subject matter. Write the page numbers and specific topics you want to go back to in the back of the book for future reference. Allow the book to be a living conversation for you. If you have a close friend, consider reading a book chapter by chapter together, and then discuss what you are reading each time.

Feedback from wise people is a means of becoming more attentive to our blind spot and new behaviors is a means of improving. The more we are aware of our healthy and unhealthy relational patterns, we can identify the growth opportunities we have and people we need to connect within the process. Out of this time, you might even consider making a list of your current life patterns you would like to both change and improve. Then start to make conscious choices about those life patterns and have a brother hold you accountable. Abandon the patterns that don't contribute to your advancement and health and build on the patterns that do.

Reflection & Mentorship

Begin

- Great men give full attention to their spiritual lives and respond to the ongoing need for growth in a world that consumes the attention of men.

Unpack

- Do you agree or disagree that men today are consumed with recreation and technology, but fail to engage with others spiritually? What evidence can you point to in support of your position?
- Are the problems men, the world, the church, or all the above?

Inform

- Proverbs 4:20 reads, *"My son, be attentive to my words; incline your ear to my sayings."* Are men no longer attentive to God's Word?

- How do we *"incline our ears"* to the truth? Explain this phrase practically.

Land

- How can you become fully engaged?
- How can you have better conversations?
- How can you place yourself around wiser men?

Do

- What do you need to do immediately?
- Submit yourself to that act of change.

Life After the Shenanigans

Life has no blessing like a prudent friend.

EURIPIDES

Men in our culture are typically great at connecting with other guys around activities like pick-up basketball, rock climbing, drinking, or drumming up a little mischief. But we are not typically great at building friendships around anything meaningful, things that promote real conversation, and getting to know each other on a deeper level. Eventually, we outgrow the shenanigans and maybe the drinking, and at some point our bodies will struggle to handle the athletic competition and physically demanding outings. What then? How will we build friendships? Are we destined for a life devoid of any brotherly camaraderie?

My assumption, of course, is that you agree with me that guys need friends who are guys. Our male friends watch our backs and cheer us on. They broaden our perspective, offer advice, and hold us accountable. They listen to our problems and walk beside us through our difficulties. They understand because they're men, and often they've "been there and done that." And we can do the same for them. No, I don't believe I need to convince you that guys need guy friends. But I will offer a couple of suggestions that I pray will help you build the sort of life-long, man-to-man friendships that will stand you in good stead for years to come.

One | Try to build better relationships with your dad and/or son(s).

"When the time drew near for David to die, he gave a charge to Solomon his son. 'I am about to go the way of all the earth,' he said. 'So be strong. Act like a man.'"

(1 Kings 2:1-2)

There's no better place to start than at home. Granted, David dropped the ball when it came to fathering, but he did have an occasional great moment, and this priceless father/son interaction was one of them. I don't mean to ignore the reality that a lot of guys face some difficult and complicated issues with their fathers or sons, but for others of us our family ties give us a natural point of entry. Our families have seen us at our best and worst, yet they love us anyway because we're family. And what a blessing it is when they get to know us well enough to appreciate who we are! Even in well-functioning families, it seems that too many of us sort of skate on the surface of our relationships. Take a chance. Break the ice. Dive deep. You might be surprised at the richness you'll discover.

Two | Take one relationship further before time passes you by.

"But woe to him who is alone when he falls and has not another to lift him up!"

(Ecclesiastes 4:10)

We've all been there; we've failed or fallen in both big and small ways. What other men in your life do you turn to when the going gets tough? Who knows you well enough to prop you up and offer just the right pep talk? With whom might you begin to build such a relationship? A co-worker?

A neighbor? A guy at church? An uncle or grandpa? Who in your life do you think you might be able to laugh with, cry with, and trust with your confidences? It takes time, effort, and intentionality to build such a friendship, so go for it. Initiate, engage, set it up: prioritize it right up there with faith, family, and job. It's too important to put off any longer.

For many of us, the biggest challenge might be just mustering the courage to put ourselves out there. It feels risky. Too many insecurities stand in the way. But with God's help, you can do this. I won't say it's easy, but I will say it's worth it.

Reflection & Mentorship

Begin

- At some point, we have to grow beyond the shenanigans and build lasting male relationships that aim to make us better men.

Unpack

- Men need some moments to be boys, but what are the limits?
- Is our search for adventure different from living a life of shenanigans?

Inform

- Read 1 Kings 2:1-2 above. What do you think David meant when he said, "act like a man?"
- What does David mean by "be strong?"
- Read Ecclesiastes 4:10. What would be the "woes" the writer infers for the man who has no friends?

Land

- What issue do you need to address in your life on this subject?
- What steps do you need to take?

Do

- Talk with a mentor about the steps you need to take immediately.

Nathan & David

Without friends no one would choose to live,
though he had all other goods.

AUGUSTINE

For some reason, it was just easier making friends when we were younger, wasn't it? We were less presumptive and more carefree. We judged people less by their status, accomplishments, and influence. We more readily laughed and were mesmerized by simple activities. Everything was a new adventure, and it was always better with a friend.

Great friendships make children better, but they make men better, too. We knew this intuitively when we were young, but for some reason as we have grown older, we have forgotten it.

In the Old Testament we are very aware that David had at least one very good friend, Jonathan. The decade of David's friendship was perhaps the most challenging, and he needed this friend to help him through. But after Jonathan was killed at war, there was another friend who stepped in, Nathan. Nathan was not so much the confidant with who he had chemistry, like Jonathan. He was more the counselor who held him accountable. But still, David's friendship-counselor relationship shaped him during his years as King of Israel.

These two men had three meetings that shape our understanding of their relationship. Each has a remarkable lesson that led to an astounding impact on the kingdom and these two men.

One | The First Move: Alliance.

Now when the king lived in his house and the Lord had given him rest from all his surrounding enemies, the king said to Nathan the prophet, "See now, I dwell in a house of cedar, but the ark of God dwells in a tent.

(2 Samuel 7:1-2)

Now when David lived in his house, David said to Nathan the prophet, "Behold, I dwell in a house of cedar, but the ark of the covenant of the Lord is under a tent." And Nathan said to David, "Do all that is in your heart, for God is with you."

(1 Chronicles 17:1-2)

This is one of those moments two men of God in two different roles came together for kingdom impact. At the end of it all, we know that David was prevented from building the house of the Lord as his hands were bloodied by war. But this did not stop David from doing everything short of building the temple. He gathered the resources, the plans, the men, and handed the baton to his son, Solomon.

In these verses, two great men, one a king and one a prophet, form an alliance. They are spiritual allies. David realizes that he has enough. He looks up at his success, security, stock, and says, "Enough." And David dreams with a Nathan about what should be done solely for the Lord.

This interaction is essential because it teaches us two things. First, it teaches us the importance of spiritual alliances with other Christian brothers.

Second, the power of two men discovering the futility of their fading glory and the importance of seeking God's glory.

Two | The Second Move: Confrontation.

But the thing that David had done displeased the Lord.
And the Lord sent Nathan to David.

(2 Samuel 11:27-12:1)

Friendship is not always easy. There are hard things we face and need to address. This moment has to be one of the top five ultimate friendship confrontations of the Bible, trumped only by Jesus' strong words to Peter, "Get behind me Satan."

The context of this confrontation is the adulterous sin of David with Bathsheba and the consequential cover-up. This one sin led to many others and a massive cover-up that David thought would protect him. However, he had not pulled one over on God. So God instructs Nathan to confront him about the sin and cover-up.

This is never an easy moment for friends. But this is what great friends do; they care enough to guide us toward Godliness and away from catastrophe. They want what God wants for us and have the courage to tell us "no" and sometimes "get right with God." Nathan does that here in 2 Samuel 12. It's worth reading.

And just when you think David could win any and every battle, this was one he was sure to lose. It's a disappointing moment for David, but one he handles well. His response to Nathan is this — "I have sinned against the LORD." (2 Samuel 12:13)

Friends have power. Never underestimate the importance of the *care-frontation.*

Three | The Third Move: Counsel.

Then Nathan said to Bathsheba the mother of Solomon,
"Have you not heard that Adonijah the son of Haggith has become
king and David our lord does not know it? Now therefore come,
let me give you advice, that you may save your own life
and the life of your son Solomon.

(1 Kings 1:11-12)

Toward the latter part of David's life, David's son Adonijah planned to forcibly take the kingdom from his father and set himself up as king. Nathan rushed to David with Bathsheba at his side to inform him of the betrayal and discuss options as his joint counsel.

There is no doubt this is not an easy moment for all three of them: a king is betrayed, a wife is at odds, and a counselor feels concern for the future of the nation. But here is the best part: they are in it together. Seeking God, his wisdom, and the best path forward, they are not alone. The resolution is to appoint Solomon as king and set up him quickly before Adonijah takes his move too far. And the plan works, but the results are still disturbing and heartbreaking. Eventually, Solomon has Adonijah executed.

We all need a man like this in our life. A man with whom we have a spiritual alliance, who can confront and counsel us. David was better for this. From this relationship came the Temple of the Lord, the repentance of a King, and the establishment of King Solomon for the next generation. Just consider the impact of not having a Nathan in your life. You might be missing out on something amazing. Don't delay! Get spiritual counsel today. Amazing benefits await.

Moses & Aaron

"Friendship is born at that moment when one person says to another, 'What! You too? I thought I was the only one.'"

C.S. LEWIS

Moses and Aaron were blood brothers, yes, but they didn't even meet until Moses was 80 years old and Aaron 83. They were fast friends from the start, though in fact, the moment Aaron first laid eyes on his younger brother, he was "glad in his heart" (Exodus 4:14). And with a little divine intervention, Aaron became Moses' spokesperson as the two of them prepared to execute the most spectacular mass escape in all of history: the exodus of Israel from Egypt. Their partnership helped initiate a whole new chapter for a nation "on the move." Here are three assets of great brothers.

One | Brothers lessen our weaknesses.

"But Moses said to the Lord, 'Oh, my Lord, I am not eloquent, either in the past or since you have spoken to your servant, but I am slow of speech and of tongue.'

"(Then the Lord) said,' Is there not Aaron, your brother, the Levite? I know that he can speak well... You shall speak to him and put the words in his mouth, and I will be with your mouth and with his

mouth and will teach you both what to do. He shall speak for you to
the people, and he shall be your mouth, and you shall be
as God to him.'"

(Exodus 4:10, 14-16)

No one knows why Moses was reluctant to speak in public. Some wonder if he was uncomfortable with a language barrier; he had grown up among Egyptian royalty, so Hebrew wouldn't have been his first language. Others speculate that he was self-conscious about some speech impediment. Whatever the reason, God appeased Moses' apprehensions by appointing Aaron to be Moses' voice, first to Pharaoh and then to the people of Israel. They complemented each other. Friends do that. They fill in each other's gaps so that together they can accomplish greater things.

Two | Brothers support through challenges.

"And the Lord said to Moses, 'See, I have made you like God to
Pharaoh, and your brother Aaron shall be your prophet. You shall
speak all that I command you, and your brother Aaron shall tell
Pharaoh to let the people of Israel go out of his land.'"

(Exodus 7:1-2)

What a boost of confidence and courage it must have been for Moses to face Pharaoh with Aaron by his side. Together they presented a united front, playing off of one another to increase their chances of a successful outcome. We know, of course, that Pharaoh never did budge, even after multiple meetings, but can you imagine what it would have been like for Moses to face Pharaoh all those times by himself? Even the mere presence of a comrade in arms can be just the encouragement we need not only to face life's challenges but also to regroup and "try, try again" as they say.

Three | Brothers are partners in ministry.

"Then bring near to you Aaron your brother, and his sons with him, from among the people of Israel, to serve me as priests—Aaron and Aaron's sons, Nadab and Abihu, Eleazar and Ithamar."

(Exodus 28:1)

Aaron had emerged as a wise and capable counselor and willing servant of the Lord, worthy of ministry leadership. His new role took his partnership with Moses to a whole new level, and Moses willingly embraced this next assignment from God for his brother and dear friend. Friends should always be cheering each other on. They take joy in their respective gifts and in seeing each other excel in their unique way.

Moses had already led an epic life before he ever met Aaron. Then, supporting each other and holding each other up through all sorts of bumps, setbacks, and discouragements, they achieved not one but *two* remarkable feats. They rescued the people of Israel from slavery in Egypt and they set them up to enter the Promised Land.

It's bittersweet that Aaron died along the way and Moses never got to cross the border, but what a journey. It's amazing what a couple of brothers in the Lord can achieve for the Kingdom when they embrace their friendship and partner in ministry.

Reflection & Mentorship

Begin

- Consider the three assets of having a brother like Moses and Aaron

Unpack

- What are some of the natural benefits of having a spiritual brother?
- What are some of the spiritual benefits of having a spiritual brother?

Inform

- Moses and Aaron were natural and spiritual brothers through a challenging journey. Based on the verses above, how did they support one another?
- Which one of these three points do you need right now in your life?

Land

- What steps do you need to take today to either find a brother or be a brother?

Do

- Take one of your selected steps today, without haste.

Paul & Barnabas

"The pain of parting is nothing to the joy of meeting again."

CHARLES DICKENS

When people think of the friendship between Paul and Barnabas, their thoughts often turn immediately to the sad break up between these two friends. The rift, of course, occurred when Barnabas proposed that his cousin Mark accompany them on their second missionary journey, but Paul opposed the idea. Their falling out was painful, and significant in part because of how deep their bond had been. They had been the best of friends and brothers.

Here are four great lessons we learn from the friendship between Paul and Barnabas.

One | Friends champion each other.

"And when he (Paul) had come to Jerusalem, he attempted to join the disciples. And they were all afraid of him, for they did not believe that he was a disciple. But Barnabas took him and brought him to the apostles and declared to them how on the road he had seen the Lord, who spoke to him, and how at Damascus he had preached boldly in the name of Jesus."

(Acts 9:26-27)

One can understand why the apostles were suspicious of Paul at first. Before his conversion, he had been a cruel persecutor of Christ-followers. But Barnabas believed that Paul's newfound devotion to Jesus and his zeal for the gospel were genuine. So he championed Paul, and because so many looked up to Barnabas, many Christian men listened to Barnabas' recommendation. Indeed, through much of Luke's account in the first half of the Book of Acts, Paul and Barnabas were inseparable. Reading between the lines, it would even seem that Barnabas played a massive role in mentoring Paul and developing his spiritual life as their friendship took root and grew.

Two | Friends partner in mission and adventure.

"While they (prophets and teachers in the church at Antioch) were worshiping the Lord and fasting, the Holy Spirit said, 'Set apart for me Barnabas and Saul (Paul) for the work to which I have called them.' Then after fasting and praying they laid their hands on them and sent them off."

(Acts 13:2-3)

Paul and Barnabas made quite a team during what we have come to call Paul's first missionary journey. They effectively communicated the gospel to audiences from the port city of Antioch to the island of Cyprus (Barnabas' home), to Asia Minor and beyond. They apparently played off of each other well, Paul was an engaging speaker and Barnabas was a born encourager (his name means "exhorter" and "comforter"). They knew each other's strengths and allowed these strengths to shine. Along the way, they encountered—and by the Holy Spirit's power defeated—an evil sorcerer, performed miracles of healing, and at one point were even mistaken for Greek gods. The response to their message and their chemistry as friends and colleagues was hugely positive, though some among their Jewish listeners were becoming a bit unnerved.

Three | Friends see each other through adversity.

"...it has seemed good to us, having come to one accord, to choose men and send them to you with our beloved Barnabas and Paul, men who have risked their lives for the name of our Lord Jesus Christ."

(Acts 15:25-26)

In this excerpt from a letter to Gentile believers from the Jerusalem Council, Paul and Barnabas are acknowledged as "men who have risked their lives for the name of our Lord Jesus Christ." The duo's encounters with the opposition during the first missionary journey were sometimes frightening, to say the least: Paul was even stoned and left for dead when they were in Lystra. But in an early demonstration of "no man left behind," Paul was rescued, and the pair hightailed it to Derbe. The point is: friends have each other's backs. They're willing to face risky, even life-threatening, ventures as a team because they know they're in it together.

Four | Friends weather their conflicts and move on.

"And after some days Paul said to Barnabas, 'Let us return and visit the brothers in every city where we proclaimed the word of the Lord, and see how they are.' Now Barnabas wanted to take with them John called Mark. But Paul thought best not to take with them one who had withdrawn from them in Pamphylia and had not gone with them to the work. And there arose a sharp disagreement, so that they separated from each other. Barnabas took Mark with him and sailed away to Cyprus, but Paul chose Silas and departed, having been commended by the brothers to the grace of the Lord. And he went through Syria and Cilicia, strengthening the churches."

(Acts 15:36-41)

This is heartbreaking. But let's make a couple of critical observations. First, the dispute between Paul and Barnabas was not about doctrine. They remained united on the gospel message and teachings of Christ they shared throughout the land. And second, they did not allow their disagreement to deter them from their mission: both went on to follow through on the work they'd committed themselves to complete. Nor is there any evidence that they bad-mouthed one another after going their separate ways. In fact, there is some indication that they eventually reconciled (see 1 Corinthians 9:6).

The truth is that conflict is inevitable even in the healthiest of relationships. It's a fact of life and certainly should never dissuade us from pursuing friendships with other brothers in the Lord. When conflict happens, we should strive not to let our tempers control our speech, and we must always seek reconciliation. In the meantime, let's take a cue from Paul and Barnabas and cheer each other on, partner with each other for the cause of Christ, and leave no man behind.

Reflection & Mentorship

Begin

- Remember the three attributes of the spiritual friendship between Paul and Barnabas.

Unpack

- What are some attributes of a great friendship?
- Not all friendships last forever. Are there good reasons that friendships don't last forever?

Inform

- Of the three points above about Paul and Barnabas' friendship, which convicts you the most? Why?

- Even though their relationship came to a natural end, was this necessarily bad?

Land

- Are there friendships you need to address?
- Do you need to start new ones, or end old ones?
- What steps do you need to take?

Do

- Take a step to address your need for great friends.

Shadrach, Meshach, & Abednego

The steady discipline of intimate friendship with Jesus
results in men becoming like Him.

HARRY EMERSON FOSDICK

The subject of many a children's song and story is the account of
Shadrach, Meshach, and Abednego. The Old Testament's Book of
Daniel is rich with lessons for God's children of all ages, and instructive
for brothers in Christ. Three young Jewish men, united in their faith and
devotion to the one true God, defied King Nebuchadnezzar's command to
bow down before a golden image he'd erected. The consequences? Death by
fire in a giant furnace.

One | Together Challenged.

> *"Then Nebuchadnezzar in furious rage commanded that Shadrach,*
> *Meshach, and Abednego be brought. So they brought these men*
> *before the king. Nebuchadnezzar answered and said to them, 'Is it*
> *true, O Shadrach, Meshach, and Abednego, that you do not serve my*
> *gods or worship the golden image that I have set up?'"*

(Daniel 3:13-14)

Together these three men stood united in their love for God and in their conviction that they should neither serve nor worship any other god but the God. We are not alone, brothers. In a world (and culture) that grows increasingly hostile toward followers of Christ, we know that we can stand firm with others who know the truth of God's Word. The unity these young men demonstrated must have impressed King Nebuchadnezzar, and perhaps even intimidated him. But their aim was not to impress or intimidate. Instead, they simply wanted to stay true to what they knew was right no matter how difficult or deadly the challenges they might face as a result.

Two | Together Resolute.

> "Shadrach, Meshach, and Abednego answered and said to the king, 'O Nebuchadnezzar, we have no need to answer you in this matter. If this be so, our God whom we serve is able to deliver us from the burning fiery furnace, and he will deliver us out of your hand, O king. But if not, be it known to you, O king, that we will not serve your gods or worship the golden image that you have set up.'"

(Daniel 3:16-18)

Interestingly, this incident involved three men and not just one. Would each of them as individuals have been able to remain so unwavering in his stance? I suspect the answer is yes, but still, what a demonstration of the support we as brothers in Christ can offer each other in the face of adversity. Whatever we face, we're in it together. We bolster each other's courage, reaffirming, and reinforcing our convictions about what is right and true. It's easier to be resolute about your position when other guys stand with you.

Three | Together Rescued.

> "Then Nebuchadnezzar came near to the door of the burning fiery furnace; he declared, 'Shadrach, Meshach, and Abednego, servants

of the Most High God, come out, and come here!' Then Shadrach,
Meshach, and Abednego came out from the fire. And the satraps, the
prefects, the governors, and the king's counselors gathered together and
saw that the fire had not had any power over the bodies of those men.
The hair of their heads was not singed, their cloaks were not harmed,
and no smell of fire had come upon them."

(Daniel 3:26-27)

What a testimony it is to God's power when we step into the fire, and he
displays his glory. If just one of the three had emerged from the furnace
unscathed, the king and his entourage might have tried to explain it away
as a fluke of airflow (or something). But all three? Not only did this trio
of friends share a remarkable life experience, but they also ended up with
quite a story to tell their families and others about God's power and how he
works in, through, and around us.

Four | Together Revered.

"Therefore I make a decree: Any people, nation, or language that
speaks anything against the God of Shadrach, Meshach, and
Abednego shall be torn limb from limb, and their houses laid in
ruins, for there is no other god who is able to rescue in this way."

(Daniel 3:29)

United they stood, unwavering in their faith, and through their steadfastness,
God changed an evil king's heart. Our relationships as brothers in Christ
are not just about what deep, meaningful friendships can mean for
us personally. They are also about how our unity influences others and
ultimately, the honor we bring to God. The victory is his, and so is the
glory.

Reflection & Mentorship

Begin

- Brotherhood is a place that spiritual brothers face challenges together.

Unpack

- Have you been through a challenge alone? What was the challenge, and how did this feel?
- Have you been through a challenge with a spiritual brother? How was this different?

Inform

- There are four scriptures and four points above. Which one do you need to hear right now?
- Why?

Land

- What issue do you need to address?
- What steps do you need to take today and this week?

Do

- Take immediate action.

David & Jonathan

At times our own light goes out and is rekindled by a spark
from another person. Each of us has cause to think with deep
gratitude of those who have lighted the flame within us.

ALBERT SCHWEITZER

As male friendships go, few can compare to the relationship between David and Jonathan. The emphasis of their relationship was a major theme throughout much of 1 Samuel in the Old Testament. The brotherhood they shared was based on love. The Hebrew word for love, which describes a platonic affection with clear political and diplomatic implications, ran deep between them and served as an example of the biblical brand of male bonding that every brother would do well to embrace—and be blessed to experience.

> *"As soon as he had finished speaking to Saul, the soul of Jonathan was knit to the soul of David, and Jonathan loved him as his own soul."*

(1 Samuel 18:1)

In the context of the Bible, to love others as you love yourself means that the other person's needs, desires, hopes, and dreams matter to you. You care about the other guy's health and well-being. And though David and Jonathan both led their own lives, they also both served the same king

(Jonathan's father Saul), the same army, and the same God. What critical principles of friendship can we learn from this extraordinary "knitting of the souls"?

One | Personal Sacrifice.

> *"Then Jonathan made a covenant with David,*
> *because he loved him as his own soul. And Jonathan stripped himself*
> *of the robe that was on him and gave it to David, and his armor,*
> *and even his sword and his bow and his belt. And David went out*
> *and was successful wherever Saul sent him, so that Saul set him over*
> *the men of war. And this was good in the sight of all the people*
> *and also in the sight of Saul's servants."*
>
> (1 Samuel 18:3-5)

That Jonathan gave his robe, armor, sword, bow, and belt to David not only demonstrates the sacrificial love, Jonathan had for his friend, but it also symbolizes a major component of their covenant: that when David succeeded Jonathan's father Saul as king of Israel, Jonathan would serve as his second in command. This was a symbol of genuine servitude and was a powerful gesture considering that the natural line of succession to the throne would have made Jonathan king. Real friends are willing to make sacrifices for each other, make plans together, and serve one another with respect and humility.

Two | Unity in Faith.

> *"Jonathan said to the young man who carried his armor, 'Come, let*
> *us go over to the garrison of these uncircumcised. It may be that the*
> *Lord will work for us, for nothing can hinder the Lord from saving*
> *by many or by few.'"*
>
> (1 Samuel 14:6)

*"Then David said to the Philistine, 'You come to me with a sword
and with a spear and with a javelin, but I come to you in the name
of the Lord of hosts, the God of the armies of Israel,
whom you have defied.'"*

1 Samuel 17:45

Both David and Jonathan were motivated by their devotion to God and
their commitment to further His kingdom. They were united in their faith,
and faithful to their callings. As in marriage, shared faith plays a huge role
in a successful relationship, partnership in mission, and ministry.

Three | Enduring Loyalty.

*"Then Saul's anger was kindled against Jonathan, and he said to
him, 'You son of a perverse, rebellious woman, do I not know that
you have chosen the son of Jesse to your own shame, and to the shame
of your mother's nakedness? For as long as the son of Jesse lives on the
earth, neither you nor your kingdom shall be established. Therefore
send and bring him to me, for he shall surely die.' Then Jonathan
answered Saul his father, 'Why should he be put to death? What has
he done?' But Saul hurled his spear at him to strike him. So Jonathan
knew that his father was determined to put David to death. And
Jonathan rose from the table in fierce anger and ate no food the
second day of the month, for he was grieved for David,
because his father had disgraced him."*

(1 Samuel 20:30-34)

The friendship between David and Jonathan had become complicated
because Jonathan's father Saul had grown to despise David and for all kinds
of reasons. Can you imagine Jonathan's predicament? He was torn between

loyalty to his father and loyalty to his friend. But Jonathan sided with David because he knew that his father's position was unjust and influenced by all kinds of wrong motives. At the risk of his own life, Jonathan maintained covert contact with David so that he could warn him of impending danger. Defending and protecting (sometimes at great risk) is what true friends do for each other.

Four | Emotional Connection.

> *"...David got up from the south side of the stone and bowed down before Jonathan three times, with his face to the ground. Then they kissed each other and wept together—but David wept the most."*

(1 Samuel 20:41)

Things with Saul had deteriorated to the point where David's life was in constant danger. It was time for him to disappear, and when the two friends had to say goodbye, they didn't know if they'd ever see each other again. One way you know you really love somebody is when it hurts so bad to part ways that the dam breaks and the tears flow. Is it worth it? Absolutely, brother. Don't let anybody tell you differently.

A friendship between men like the one David and Jonathan shared is all too rare. My prayer, guys, is that the Lord will bless every one of us with such a bond of brotherhood.

Reflection & Mentorship

Begin

- Friendship pays out incredible dividends in a man's life if we work at staying in a relationship.

Unpack

- Many male friendships often lack the needed work and effort. Why do women do this naturally, yet men don't?

Inform

- Which of the scripture references above are important for you to hear right now in your life?
- Why?

Land

- Which one of the four points about David and Jonathan's friendship is something you need or something you need to do?

Do

- Be a better friend today.

Paul & Timothy

A true friend is the greatest of all blessings.

FRANCOIS DE LA ROCHEFOUCAULD

Paul and Timothy shared a deep friendship and a productive partnership in the faith. Several passages of Scripture in the New Testament bear witness to the evolution of their brotherhood and mentorship. It was a relationship that resulted in significant spiritual impact, one that advanced the gospel from mentor to protégé and from one generation to the next. Here is the progression and impact.

One | Fathering in the Faith.

"To Timothy, my true child in the faith: Grace, mercy, and peace from God the Father and Christ Jesus our Lord."

(1 Timothy 1:2)

Timothy's father was Greek, and his mother Eunice was a Jew who later decided to follow Jesus. Her mother Lois, Timothy's grandmother, also came to know the Lord. Scholars believe both women were converted during Paul's first visit to their home city of Lystra (Acts 14). The influence of these two women in Timothy's life laid a strong foundation for what was to come later, as Paul himself noted: "...from childhood you have been acquainted with the sacred writings, which are able to make you wise for salvation through faith in Christ Jesus." (2 Tim. 3:15)

It was right after he began his second missionary journey that Paul met Timothy and, upon the recommendation of several church leaders in Lystra, invited him to accompany him on his travels. From the very start, Paul is attentively and spiritually "parenting" Timothy. He brought Timothy alongside him to share in his day-to-day experiences; essentially, the two men "did life together" for several years. Timothy was heavily involved in Paul's subsequent missionary journeys, as well.

Paul was about 15 years older than Timothy, and it was apparent that he took the responsibility of being a role model of faith for the younger man seriously. Still, the two men also shared a genuine affection for each other, forged in day-to-day, real events. Timothy observed Paul's character and conduct in all kinds of circumstances and in the process the seeds his mentor planted began to sprout tangible, valuable fruit. Paul came to trust Timothy implicitly, and would send him as his emissary when needed, confident of the reception he would receive: "But you know Timothy's proven worth, how as a son with a father he has served with me in the gospel." (Philippians 2:22)

Two | Following in the Faith.

> *"You, however, have followed my teaching, my conduct,*
> *my aim in life, my faith, my patience, my love, my steadfastness, my*
> *persecutions and sufferings that happened to me at Antioch,*
> *at Iconium, and at Lystra – which persecutions I endured; yet from*
> *them all the Lord rescued me."*

(2 Timothy 3:10-11)

Throughout the years, as the friendship between Paul and Timothy evolved, the two shared both highs (seeing many come to Christ and the growth of new churches) and lows (illness, physical dangers, persecutions, and Paul's imprisonment). They became partners in sharing the gospel, and God used their collaboration to accomplish much toward building His kingdom. The Bible indicates Timothy was directly involved in the ministry of at least five New Testament churches (I Thessalonians 3; 1 Corinthians 4; Philippians 2; Acts 17; I Timothy 3). Their travels took them far and wide, from Rome, throughout Macedonia, all over Asia, and to Jerusalem.

Three | Fellow-working in the Faith.

"Timothy, my fellow worker, greets you; so do Lucius and Jason and Sosipater, my kinsmen."

(Romans 16:21)

From son to student to peer and fellow laborer in service to the Kingdom, Timothy made measurable, visible progress, becoming a strong man of God. But it didn't just happen. By intentionally pouring time and effort into Timothy, Paul followed the example Jesus modeled with each of His disciples, investing in the relationship with a purpose. Ephesians 4 makes it clear that Jesus always sought to develop the God-given potential of those He was teaching and leading. "He who descended is the one who also ascended far above all the heavens, that he might fill all things. And he gave the apostles, the prophets, the evangelists, the shepherds and teachers, to equip the saints for the work of ministry, for building up the body of Christ, until we all attain to the unity of the faith and of the knowledge of the Son of God, to mature manhood, to the measure of the stature of the fullness of Christ..." (Ephesians 4:10-13)

We are called to become more like Jesus and to encourage others to do the same in order that we all will be able to use our God-given gifts and abilities for their God-given purpose. When he saw the end of his life on earth drawing near Paul "passed his mantle" of ministry on to the person he knew would continue the ministry of the good news of Christ. "I charge you in the presence of God and of Christ Jesus, who is to judge the living and the dead, and by his appearing and his kingdom: preach the word; be ready in season and out of season; reprove, rebuke, and exhort, with complete patience and teaching." (2 Timothy 4:1-2) He had experienced great joy and rewards in helping someone become the person God intended him to be—and so will we if we do the same, purposefully.

"Therefore encourage one another and build one another up, just as you are doing."

(I Thess. 5:11)

Reflection & Mentorship

Build

- From mentor to protégé, we can leave a spiritual impact on the next generation.

Unpack

- Who is someone who has had an impact on your life?
- Describe one thing they did to make a real difference.

Inform

- Of the scriptures above, which one captured your attention? Why?
- What does this scripture teach about the benefits or impact of brotherhood and mentorship?

Land

- What one person do you need to invest in today?
- How would their life and outcomes look different if you did?

Do

- Call the person mentioned above and schedule a meet-up.

Moses & Jethro

Better is open rebuke than hidden love. Faithful are the
wounds of a friend; profuse are the kisses of an enemy.

PROVERBS 27:5-6

J ethro was Moses' father-in-law, but more than that, he was Moses'
brother in the Lord and friend. Day in and day out, they lived and
worked alongside each other as Moses guided Israel to the Promised
Land. Ponder the passage of Scripture in Exodus in which Jethro initiates
a little "conference" between the two men that forever influences the way
Moses conducts his daily responsibilities as Israel's God-appointed leader
through the desert wilderness:

> *The next day Moses sat to judge the people, and the people stood
> around Moses from morning till evening. When Moses' father-in-law
> saw all that he was doing for the people, he said, "What is this that
> you are doing for the people? Why do you sit alone, and all the people
> stand around you from morning till evening?" And Moses said to
> his father-in-law, "Because the people come to me to inquire of God;
> when they have a dispute, they come to me and I decide between one
> person and another, and I make them know the statutes of God and
> his laws." Moses' father-in-law said to him, "What you are doing is
> not good. You and the people with you will certainly wear yourselves
> out, for the thing is too heavy for you. You are not able to do it alone.*

*Now obey my voice; I will give you advice, and God be with you! You
shall represent the people before God and bring their cases to God,
and you shall warn them about the statutes and the laws, and make
them know the way in which they must walk and what they must do.
Moreover, look for able men from all the people, men who fear God,
who are trustworthy and hate a bribe, and place such men over the
people as chiefs of thousands, of hundreds, of fifties, and of tens. And
let them judge the people at all times. Every great matter they shall
bring to you, but any small matter they shall decide themselves. So it
will be easier for you, and they will bear the burden with you. If you
do this, God will direct you, you will be able to endure, and all this
people also will go to their place in peace."*

(Exodus 18:13-23)

Notice three ways that Jethro's counsel demonstrated his love for Moses
and his concern for Moses' welfare:

One | Observe and ask good questions.

*"What is this that you are doing for the people? Why do you sit alone,
and all the people stand around you from morning till evening?"*

(Exodus 18:14)

While the number of people exiting Egypt is up for some debate, we know
that around a million Israelites made this divine departure. Can you imagine
the multitude of disputes that must have arisen each day as this nomadic
band wandered through the hot, dusty desert? Moses found himself having
to hear and make judgments about myriad conflicts big and small, and
it occupied an excessive amount of his time. Enter an older, wiser friend
(who apparently was also a prince of a father-in-law) who'd seen enough
and decided the time was right to pose a couple of pointed questions. Great

questions drive great discussions, and thoughtful, observant friends come armed with queries that are at once sensitive, relevant, and constructive.

Two | Offer caring observations.

"What you are doing is not good. You and the people with you will certainly wear yourselves out, for the thing is too heavy for you. You are not able to do it alone.

(Exodus 18:17-18)

I don't believe Jethro intended his observations to be critical of Moses or an allusion to some inadequacy in the quality of the leadership he was providing. On the contrary, I believe Jethro had had enough life experience to know that no man—no matter how capable—could maintain the pace that Moses had been keeping. He was concerned that his daughter's husband would eventually wear himself out, not only damaging his health but also undermining his effectiveness as a leader. In fact, I think there was a hint of admiration and affirmation in Jethro's remarks. "You're doing a great job," he seemed to be saying. "Let's just make sure you can keep on keeping on." Jethro's motive was to safeguard Moses' welfare. He was looking after his friend.

Three | Make suggestions on how to do it better.

Moreover, look for able men from all the people, men who fear God, who are trustworthy and hate a bribe, and place such men over the people as chiefs of thousands, of hundreds, of fifties, and of tens. And let them judge the people at all times. Every great matter they shall bring to you, but any small matter they shall decide themselves. So it will be easier for you, and they will bear the burden with you.

(Exodus 18:21-22)

The voice of experience! Sound advice from a wise elder: delegate and share the load! Excellent counsel for any of us, yes, but the point here is that Jethro didn't just leave Moses hanging with a string of critical comments. He also offered solid suggestions for doing things in a different, potentially better way. Constructive criticism is pretty worthless unless accompanied by a workable solution or two.

Perhaps you are the friend who is concerned about a brother and his welfare. Your task, then, is not to judge or condescend. Instead, it is to ask thoughtful questions, offer honest observations, and propose workable solutions in a sensitive, loving way. Or maybe you are the recipient of such input from a trusted friend. Your response should be to listen with a humble heart and receive your brother's words with an attitude of gratitude. Even if your brother's comments seem somewhat off base or a little offensive, humility and gratitude are still the order of the day. (Especially if the friend happens to be your father-in-law!)

Reflection & Mentorship

Begin

- Great friends and fathers find ways to influence and care for the welfare and future of others.

Unpack

- Regardless of whether or not you are a father-in-law or not, is it hard to offer advice to a son-in-law? Why?
- Do we need to overcome this concern before it becomes apathetic? If so, how?

Inform

- Of the three points which one stands out to you?

- What from the corresponding text challenges you, or what insights do you gain?

Land

- What is one action you need to take immediately?

Do

- Take action and share your experience with a friend or mentor.

Beyond Perceptions

If two friends ask you to judge a dispute, don't accept,
because you will lose one friend; on the other hand, if two
strangers come with the same request, accept, because you
will gain one friend.

AUGUSTINE

H ave you noticed how often men in TV sitcoms today are the butt of
jokes because of the perceived frailties and inadequacies our culture
loves to target? The jokes get laughs because on some level (sad to
say) there's some truth to them. But among our purposes as followers of
Jesus Christ is to represent him to the world. Now get this: Jesus is the
finest example of what a real man should be. He's our ultimate model and
mentor. He's the one we want to emulate. And as we grow in righteousness,
becoming more and more like Him, we have a golden opportunity to
demonstrate to our culture—indeed to the world—what God intended men
to be from the start. So let's look at three key ways we can live beyond
popular perceptions and demonstrate to the world how real men live life.

One | Live beyond male self-interest.

"Therefore it says, 'God opposes the proud,
but gives grace to the humble.'"

(James 4:6)

Proud. Boastful. Arrogant. Tending to "toot one's own horn." Do you know guys like that? Are you maybe a little like that yourself? As believers, humility should be among our axioms. I'm willing to bet that the men you most admire are more modest than immodest. Braggarts are annoying, and in the long run, repelling. So let it be our aim to express sincere interest in the other guy. Let's defeat the temptation to be sure everyone knows about our accomplishments and good qualities, and focus instead on the other guy's story. Yes, we want to be ready to relate our account the moment an opportunity presents itself: the story of our redemption in Christ and what He's done for us, and also the story of how the truth of his gospel has transformed our lives. But that's all about Jesus, and it's not about us. It's about what Jesus accomplished for us on the cross. Never forget these words:

> *"For by grace, you have been saved through faith.*
> *And this is not your own doing; it is the gift of God, not a result*
> *of works, so that no one may boast. For we are his workmanship,*
> *created in Christ Jesus for good works, which God prepared*
> *beforehand, that we should walk in them."*

(Ephesians 2:8-10)

Two | Live beyond male competitiveness.

> *"And the Lord's servant must not be quarrelsome but kind to*
> *everyone, able to teach, patiently enduring evil, correcting his*
> *opponents with gentleness."*

(2 Timothy 2:24)

Competition is one way we, as men, enjoy life. Whether in sports on the field or board games around the kitchen table, competition is a form of entertainment we can understand and use to get to know one another.

Frequently in the working world, we encounter a little friendly competition when we hope to land that next promotion or position. And that's okay. But even though we may engage in or face a bit of good-natured competition from time to time, let's be sure we don't let the spirit of competition dictate our attitudes or posturing with others. Humility, kindness, teaching, and sometimes even providing correction with patience and gentleness—this is the way of Christ. It ought to be our way, too.

Three | Live beyond male insecurity.

"He drew me up from the pit of destruction, out of the miry bog, and set my feet upon a rock, making my steps secure."
(Psalm 40:2)

We have more reason for security than any man who does not know Christ because we have found real security in a saving God. Let's keep in mind who we are in Jesus: children of our heavenly Father and co-heirs with the Son, the Prince of Peace. We know that we will spend eternity with him in Paradise. Nothing can take that away from us: no, failure, no setback, no illness, no difficulty in our lives can separate us from His love. So let's lay our insecurities at the feet of Jesus and live like we really believe the truth about our security in Him.

> *"If God is for us, who can be against us? He who did not spare his own Son but gave him up for us all, how will he not also with him graciously give us all things? Who shall bring any charge against God's elect? It is God who justifies. Who is to condemn? Christ Jesus is the one who died—more than that, who was raised—who is at the right hand of God, who indeed is interceding for us. Who shall separate us from the love of Christ? Shall tribulation, or distress, or persecution, or famine, or nakedness, or danger, or sword? As it is written, 'For your sake we are being killed all the day long; we are regarded as sheep to be slaughtered.'*

"No, in all these things we are more than conquerors through him who loved us. For I am sure that neither death nor life, nor angels nor rulers, nor things present nor things to come, nor powers, nor height nor depth, nor anything else in all creation, will be able to separate us from the love of God in Christ Jesus our Lord."

(Romans 8:31-39)

There is so much more, of course, to living beyond the world's misperceptions of what it means to be a man. But we can start with these. We can do it all with the help of the Holy Spirit, and the support of a brother or two in Christ who will encourage us and hold us accountable. So live beyond, and as I always say, live *all in.*

Reflection & Mentorship

Begin

- In this world, the Christian man should live beyond the usual perceptions of males.

Unpack

- Do men get a bad rap today just for being men?
- Why is this so?

Inform

- Of the points made above, which of these scriptures strike you as most relevant in your situation?
- What truth does this scripture teach?

Land

- What actionable steps do you need to take?
- Are there any obstacles you anticipate?

Do

- Take one step and report back to a friend or mentor what happened.

Build Emotional Disclosure

The Lord tests the righteous, but his soul hates the wicked
and the one who loves violence.

(PSALM 11:5)

For God so loved the world that he gave his only Son,
that whoever believes in him should not perish
but have eternal life.

(JOHN 3:16)

It's okay to have emotions. God made us that way. He created us in his image, and even God expresses emotion, as we see above. So despite anything you may have come to believe as a man in our culture, we have God's green light not only to experience emotions but also to express the emotion we feel as well. We need to move beyond being emotionless, single-dimensional, stoic men. So let's start now to make life a little more interesting.

One | Move beyond anger.

*"I desire then that in every place the men should pray,
lifting holy hands without anger or quarreling."*

(1 Timothy 2:8)

Anger often comes to mind as the first and only acceptable emotion of men. It may be the only emotion we know, and for some men, it's a biggie. Irritation, frustration, and aggravation: all might be considered variations of this one emotion. And while anger is not taboo (remember: Jesus cleared the temple of money changers), it's undoubtedly an emotion we must learn to control and express constructively as we mature in Christ.

But my purpose in addressing this is not to analyze or provide therapy for any emotions that might challenge or govern us. Instead, I want us to acknowledge and embrace the full range of emotions with which God has blessed us. One psychologist and researcher suggests there are only eight basic emotions. Others list 400 or more (Wow!). Regardless, I believe that we shortchange ourselves and hold ourselves back until we learn to identify, acknowledge, and manage in Christlike ways all of our emotions. It's time to become the full dimensional and emotion bearing men God created us to be.

Two | Get in touch with your positive emotions.

"But the fruit of the Spirit is love, joy, peace, patience, kindness, goodness, faithfulness, gentleness, self-control; against such things there is no law."

(Galatians 5:22-23)

There have been times when it was considered less than "macho" to have any sympathetic feelings at all. Men had those feelings, of course, but hid them or contained them. And I believe these misconceptions about masculinity linger in many circles even today. As men we need to mature beyond this.

We should allow ourselves to feel and express sadness and not be ashamed of such feelings, not hide them. We should allow ourselves to experience joy and not be ashamed of feeling this way. The truth is, we *do* experience and at times should express these sympathetic and empathetic emotions. At the same time, though, we must ask ourselves if these emotions are triggered by a natural prompting or a spiritual prompting. For when the Holy Spirit prompts a man, God will capitalize on our connection with him to produce the "fruits of the spirit," we see listed above in Galatians. Let's be sure that (1) our "objects of affection" inventory is healthy and biblically permissible, and that (2) Jesus is at the top of it.

Three | Go to God to more deeply understand your emotional self.

"Let my cry come before you, O Lord; give me understanding according to your word!"

(Psalm 119:169)

One might consider David (the primary author of the Psalms) to be the ultimate "macho man." After all, he slew giant Goliath with only shepherd's tools, didn't he? But for him, there was no holding back when it came to expressing his emotions to God. He cried out to God in anger, sorrow, fear, and often utter joy. We should follow his lead and start with the Lord. We have a no holds barred relationship with God, and we should express emotion to him. David did. Scream in pain, shout in anger, cry in grief, and sing for joy. Anything goes. Nothing we can say to Him will diminish his unconditional love for us. We can be totally honest with him, even when he might be the object of our anger rather than the object of our affection! The truth is He loves us, regardless. He loves it when we are genuine with him and pour out with total transparency whatever is on our hearts.

There's a sense of unprecedented freedom when we learn to identify and express our emotions. But there's still an element of discipline to it as well. God gives us the latitude to rant and rave at him all we want, but we must endeavor to be like Christ when we express our emotions (negative or positive) to another individual. There's a learning curve, yes, but it's worth the effort, lest we remain mere one-dimensional emotional men. Anger is not your only emotion.

Reflection & Mentorship

Begin

- Men must build emotional disclosure and get in touch with emotions beyond anger.

Unpack

- Is it true that men hide or conceal their emotions?
- Why is this so?

Inform

- Of the points made above, which convicts you the most?
- What truth does this scripture teach you?

Land

- What steps do you need to take to build emotional disclosure?
- What issues do you think you will encounter?

Do

- Try sharing emotionally with someone you trust, and grow in your understanding.

6 Reasons Why Guys Need Guy Friends

Most every culture in the world recognizes the value of friendship. Literature abounds with quotes on the subject.

> "But friendship is precious, not only in the shade, but in the sunshine of life."

THOMAS JEFFERSON

> "The bird a nest, the spider a web, man, friendship."

WILLIAM BLAKE

So why is it that in our modern culture so many men shortchange themselves when it comes to developing deep friendships? Perhaps we fail to recognize just how we are enriched by truly connecting with men of faith that God brings into our lives? Here are six things we miss out on if we don't nurture healthy friendships with other guys.

1. Sharpening

"Iron sharpens iron, and one man sharpens another."

(Proverbs 27:17)

Some of the sharpening processes are intentional. We might apprentice with a friend who teaches us a new skill, or meet regularly with a brother as a mentor or mentee, or learn from a more advanced one-on-one Bible study partner. Or we may be challenged by someone we respect to see an issue from a different point of view, or to step out of our comfort zone in some way. Sometimes the sharpening is the result of healthy, good-natured competition. We tend to step up our game when in the presence of a better opponent (or a better teammate). Sometimes the sharpening happens just by doing life with and observing another brother, watching the way he interacts with others and handles challenging situations. Sharpening can change us and help us grow. We may see benefits on all levels: mentally, socially, emotionally, physically, and spiritually.

2. Companionship

"A man of many companions may come to ruin, but there is a friend who sticks closer than a brother."

(Proverbs 18:24)

Clearly, it's better to have at least one really good friend than to dabble here and there among lots of surface relationships. Even more important, though, is that we *choose* our friends well. You can either spend time with a companion whose influence makes you a better man, strengthening your faith, helping you along the way of life, or you can hang out with guys who drag you down and get you in trouble, having a detrimental impact on your character along the way.

3. Acceptance

"A friend loves at all times, and a brother is born for adversity."

(Proverbs 17:17)

How good it is to enjoy friendship with another guy who is faithful no matter how badly we screw up; someone who appreciates us flaws and all; someone who knows us well and loves us, anyway. There's nothing more healing than when a friend not only stands beside us but also helps us pick up the pieces and move on in the aftermath of disappointment or the consequences of poor choices. And likewise, *we* are better men when we demonstrate that same consideration for other brothers in our lives.

4. Accountability

"Do not be deceived: 'Bad company ruins good morals.'"

(1 Corinthians 15:33)

I admit that it sometimes hurts to be admonished by someone we love, admire, and from whom we crave approval. But of course, we do each other no favors by winking at a brother's questionable decisions or letting his sins slide by as if there's nothing wrong. What kind of love is that? I'm not saying we should be judgmental, continually pointing out another guy's weaknesses. But at the same time, really good friends will nudge each other, give each other a poke, and intervene in some way when a brother seems to be veering off-course. We want to encourage each other in loving ways to behave well and make good choices. And if you're really serious about overcoming some recurring bad habit, enter into an accountability arrangement with another guy, agreeing to check up on each other and be honest when you've stumbled, praying for each other and cheering each other on along the right path.

5. Wisdom

"Whoever walks with the wise becomes wise, but the companion of fools will suffer harm."

(Proverbs 13:20)

Again, so much rides on the company we keep. But when we walk with another man whose wisdom runs strong and deep—perhaps an older friend or mentor with a wealth of life experience and spiritual maturity—we can only benefit. We ask for wisdom, but we can't expect God to make us wise suddenly. He often grants our request through our investment of time with a well-chosen brother.

6. Encouragement

"And let us consider how to stir up one another to love and good works."

(Hebrews 10:24)

We need to be intentional about encouraging each other. It's not something we should only expect from others. We need to look for ways to encourage the other guy, to perpetuate a mutual cycle of inspiration that motivates and generates enthusiasm for really loving and serving others with joyful hearts.

So find a friend. Be a friend. Let's step further into becoming the men God designed us to be.

Reflection & Mentorship

Begin

- Guys need guy friends for all kinds of biblical reasons.

Unpack

- Why do men have so few good friends, given all the benefits?
- Or do men build all the wrong kinds of friendships?

Inform

- Which of the six scriptures above do you need to address? Why?
- What does your scripture teach you about brotherhood?

Land

- What actions can you take today?

Do

- Take action and share the result with a trusted friend or mentor.

Man Is Not Meant to Do Life Alone

God, how we get our fingers in each other's clay. That's friendship, each playing the potter to see what shapes we can make of each other.

RAY BRADBURY

Fess up if you're lonely. Really: this is too important to shrug off. Not only is loneliness a significant contributor to depression, but frequently it's a factor in suicides. Did you know that men are nearly four times more likely to die from suicide than women? That's shocking. And loneliness also is associated with obesity, high blood pressure, lowered immune rates, and other potentially lethal health issues. One can accurately say that our lack of connection with other guys may be killing us. It is slowly resulting in physical pain and death.

One | The Power of Two (Or More)

> *"Two are better than one, because they have a good reward for their toil. For if they fall, one will lift up his fellow. But woe to him who is alone when he falls and has not another to lift him up!"*

(Ecclesiastes 4:9-10)

God never intended for us to go through life or face its challenges by ourselves. Not only does he sustain us by his own power, but he also provides support through the other men he brings into our lives. Numbers 11 recounts how, when Moses found the burden of leading the contentious Israelites became too heavy for him, God directed him to gather together some of the elders and leaders so that He could empower them to help Moses as needed.

> *"They shall bear the burden of the people with you, so that you may not bear it yourself alone"*

(Numbers 11:17).

God also surrounded David with mighty warriors whose love, devotion, and help influenced his life in myriad ways (2 Samuel 23).

Two | Cultivate a Few Close Male Friends

> *"Then Jonathan made a covenant with David, because he loved him as his own soul."*

(1 Samuel 18:3)

Stories in both the Old and New Testament bear out how vital our human relationships are, and through them we learn how God has designed us for fellowship not only with Himself, but also with each other. Jesus understood that every man needs support and friendship with other men. He sought out his disciples with intentionality, quite early in his ministry (Matthew 4; Mark 1; Luke 5). Scripture makes it clear that those relationships were personal and vital to Him, not just in the context of teacher and follower. He needed them in his darkest moments in Gethsemane. He shared his heart with them daily. He referred to them not just as brothers, but also as his friends.

"No longer do I call you servants, for the servant does not know what his master is doing; but I have called you friends, for all that I have heard from my Father I have made known to you."

(John 15:15)

Three | Make It a Matter of Prayer

Finding a true friend is not always an easy task, but we owe it to ourselves to make it a priority. Bible scholars tend to single out three from among Jesus' disciples and apostles who were His closest guy friends: Peter, James, and John. Those friendships evolved as they ministered together and endured life together. So pray about it. Make it a point to identify one or two guys with whom you can nurture a healthy, biblical friendship. Male friendships provide something very different from the connection one might have with a girlfriend or a spouse, and we men can validate each other in ways that the women in our lives cannot. Some activities and experiences can only be shared with other men, a camaraderie that evolves among brothers unique to the bonds of man-to-man relationships.

Brothers, we need to acknowledge that developing friendships with other men is essential. It brings us that much closer to maturing into the men God intends us to be. We need each other. It's how He designed us. It's not a show of weakness. Instead, it's a reflection of the fellowship our triune God enjoys as Father, Son, and Holy Spirit.

And the truth is, our very lives may depend on it!

Reflection & Mentorship

Begin

- Men need other men and the friendships that come from them, for we are better together.

Unpack

- Why do men tend not to build great relationships with other men?
- What needs to be done to address this?

Inform

- Referencing John 15:15 above, how does it feel to be called a friend of God?
- What would this title infer about our relationship with God?

Land

- How would your life be spiritually changed with even one great spiritual relationship with another man? Or how has a relationship in the past impacted it?
- What steps do you need to take to forge a deeper spiritual relationship with another man?

Do

- Do something today to take action on your need for brotherhood.

Isolation Is Our Enemy

"After this there was a feast of the Jews, and Jesus went up
to Jerusalem. Now there is in Jerusalem by the Sheep Gate
a pool, in Aramaic called Bethesda, which has five roofed
colonnades. In these lay a multitude of invalids—blind, lame,
and paralyzed. One man was there who had been an invalid
for thirty-eight years. When Jesus saw him lying there and
knew that he had already been there a long time, he said to
him, "Do you want to be healed?" The sick man answered him,
"Sir, I have no one to put me into the pool when the water
is stirred up, and while I am going another steps down
before me." Jesus said to him, "Get up, take up your bed,
and walk." And at once the man was healed,
and he took up his bed and walked.

(JOHN 5:1-9)

Think about it: for 38 years, this man sat in the same spot, lonely and
tired, without a friend to help him. Can you imagine the heap of
loneliness and human pain buffeted by the surging tides of thousands
of people who failed to see him or reach out to him—for decades? But Jesus
singled him out. He connected with him as an individual. Jesus saw his
need and met it.

How often are men isolated in loneliness?

And how often is it a misery of our own making?

We do not know how many people must have suffered by the pool of Bethesda, many of them abandoned by those who should have been there for them. But sometimes we are the ones who isolate ourselves, putting up invisible walls in an effort to maintain a meaningless façade to the world, or afraid to show any vulnerability that might be perceived as a weakness. This is not how Jesus lived out his humanity. He was authentic. He was not afraid to be and reveal the man he really was. And though he would at times withdraw from others (most often to be in communion with the Father) he did not neglect to maintain friendship and fellowship with the men he had sought out to be his community. We should follow his example and seek out relationships with other men, for isolation is the enemy of men.

Here are some steps we can take as men.

One | Take a self-assessment.

> "I am like a desert owl of the wilderness, like an owl of the waste places; I lie awake; I am like a lonely sparrow on the housetop."

> (Psalm 102:6-7)

Are you prone to isolation? To being that lone wolf of a man?

I know that even I occasionally need a little solitude: time to rest, regroup, and recharge. But there's a big difference between healthy isolation and intentionally retreating into an abyss of loneliness. Do you have any guy friends you meet with regularly, not just for recreation, but to interact with about things that matter? Not just trivial stuff but some real conversations? As men, we need to strike a balance in this area; otherwise, we will discover one day we have a lot of acquaintances but not a lot of meaningful friends that help us become better men.

Two | Take stock of your current relationships.

"Do not be deceived: 'Bad company ruins good morals.'"

(1 Corinthians 15:33)

We tend to subconsciously (and sometimes consciously) adopt many of the attitudes and values of those we spend the most time with, which makes our choices when it comes to close friends more important than we realize. This doesn't mean that we spend time only with those who are just like us, but rather that we exercise discernment in the way we invest in relationships with others. We need friendships, but we need to choose wisely. We need to choose friends who will draw us closer to God, and not distance us from Him. Take some time to take stock of your relationships. Are they driving you toward good and godly things, or do most of them drive you away from godly things?

Three | Take small steps in the right direction.

"Two are better than one, because they have a good reward for their toil. For if they fall, one will lift up his fellow. But woe to him who is alone when he falls and has not another to lift him up! Again, if two lie together, they keep warm, but how can one keep warm alone? And though a man might prevail against one who is alone, two will withstand him — a threefold cord is not quickly broken."

(Ecclesiastes 4:9-12)

This passage is often quoted at weddings, but the context actually refers to all our human relationships; indeed, the verses that precede it talk about a man alone, having "neither son nor brother." God makes it clear to us: we need each other. Not only is there reward in a relationship, but we are all stronger together than we can ever be on our own.

Just as Jesus made the first move when He approached that lonely man at Bethesda; he has also made the first move with us. He lived his life on earth as he would have us live ours, focused on God while also reaching out to not only heal and teach others but also to share life with others; the ultimate act of fellowship. And then he died on the cross in our place.

May we, as he did, strike a balance between solitude and deep connection with a close, trusted brother in the Lord.

Reflection & Mentorship

Begin

- Isolation is the great enemy of all mankind. God does not want us to live in isolation from relationships.

Unpack

- Why is isolation such an issue?
- Does our busyness keep us from realizing our real need?

Inform

- Read John 5:8-9: How does this text grab you?
- How does Jesus' response grab you?

Land

- What behaviors do you need to address based on your desire to isolate yourself from relationships?

Do

- Build a new relationship today with another man or take a relationship with someone you know a little deeper.

Forging Friendships

I never considered a difference of opinion in politics, in
religion, in philosophy, as cause for withdrawing
from a friend.

THOMAS JEFFERSON

The subject of male friendships, especially the challenges men
encounter in developing them, has become a hot topic in recent years,
in both church circles and the secular world as the effects of social
isolation among us become more apparent. The issue has been addressed
in publications as diverse as the *Boston Globe* newspaper and *Men's Health*
magazine, and popular pundits raising the issue on podcasts have sparked
an outpouring of public response and debate.

But the Christian community has long been striving to shine a spotlight on
men's real (and too often neglected) needs for encouragement, fellowship,
and guidance, as evidenced by the rise in the number of men's ministry
organizations in the last three decades. Men everywhere, regardless of age,
race, background, profession, or stage of life, need each other. Though we
as believers should find it easier to connect, given that a shared faith already
unites us, it seems harder and harder to make it happen. So, how can we
effectively begin meeting our undeniable need for authentic friendships?
Here are a few suggestions.

One | Bring People Along.

"And he appointed twelve (whom he also named apostles) so that they might be with him and he might send them out to preach."

(Mark 3:14)

How do you spend your time? What are some of your interests or activities? Do you work out, bowl, golf, or shoot hoops one night a week at the gym, or do you prefer to hang out at the local coffee shop or diner? Maybe you're into music, theater, or love winning trivia contests at the local library? Whatever it is you're involved in, try bringing someone along with you. You can even drive or ride together to a men's retreat, conference, bowl game, camping trip—the possibilities are endless. The power of an invite is incredible. When men invite me places, I try to find every way possible to say yes. We get to know each other as we come alongside each other; doing something together often is the key to building a relationship.

Two | Take a Brother Out to Eat.

"Now before the Feast of the Passover, when Jesus knew that his hour had come to depart out of this world to the Father, having loved his own who were in the world, he loved them to the end."

(John 13:1)

Many a friendship begins over a plate of food. Most of us like food. Getting together for a meal is universally recognized as the form of fellowship. Some of the deepest, most meaningful conversations happen around the dining table. Occasionally it works to ask a guy over to your house for a meal. Still, unless you live alone or your wife/kids are away for a while, it's practically impossible to converse heart-to-heart in the presence of other family members. It needn't be complicated, though. Treat a guy to dinner at your favorite bar and grill. "Let's grab a burger" could be the first step on the road to building an excellent friendship.

Three | Do Great Deeds Together.

"And let us consider how to stir up one another to love and good work..."

(Hebrews 10:24)

"Greater love has no one than this, that someone lay down his life for his friends."

(John 15:13)

Our interests and activities can be springboards to making connections with others, but uniting in what we genuinely care about may forge even deeper bonds. Join with a friend to do things that you believe really matter: maybe leading a Bible study or helping with your church's youth or children's ministries. Perhaps you feel called to mentor students in an after-school program, or volunteer at the local food bank. Volunteering together for a good cause is a great way to further and nurture a friendship. You can even plan ahead and carve out some time to participate in a short-term (or long-term) inner city or overseas mission trip. Make great memories together. The most durable bonds between men are woven in the process of doing something meaningful, with a higher need-meeting, justice-serving, gospel-spreading, kingdom-building purpose.

Be creative. There are lots of ways to connect with another guy that are conducive to great fellowship and deep conversation. And be patient. Friendships take time. The *Journal of Social and Personal Relationships* estimates that, on average, it takes about 90 hours with someone before you consider him a real friend, and 200 to become a close friend. Sounds a little extreme,

I know, but the point is that building a solid friendship requires time and commitment. The result? You and your brother become more and more the men God designed you to be. Why settle for anything less?

Reflection & Mentorship

Begin

- We need to take practical action to forge new friendships.

Unpack

- Do men fail to forge friendships because we don't take the initiative, or is there another reason?

Inform

- Of the three texts above, which one convicts you the most?
- What does the scripture you choose convict you about?

Land

- What one action do you need to take to forge a new friendship today?

Do

- Don't wait one more day, forge a friendship or take one further today.

Are We Afraid of Bromance

I have friends in overalls whose friendship I would not swap
for the favor of the kings of the world.

THOMAS A. EDISON

Well, okay, by all current definitions, I suppose *bromance* might actually apply to the kind of friendship we ought to seek as brothers in Christ. In a nutshell, a bromance is a deep, non-sexual friendship between guys. One source says the word was coined in the 1990's by Dave Carnie, editor of a skateboard magazine called *Big Brother*. It's real, and it's essential. So here are three ways we can pursue the biblical brand of brotherly love.

One | Demonstrate Affection.

> *"Love one another with brotherly affection.*
> *Outdo one another in showing honor."*
>
> (Romans 12:10)

Things haven't changed. I enjoy Paul's nod in Romans 12:10 to a guy's natural inclination to compete. It was true then, and it's true now. We've learned that competition can lead to undesirable consequences when carried too far. But hey: if compete we must, why not see who can "outdo one another in showing honor"?

Brag on your brother. Build him up. Encourage him. Acknowledge and applaud his accomplishments. I'm not talking about meaningless flattery here; I'm talking about sincere praise for things that are true and things that matter, big or small.

And guys, with a measure of caution, let me say that it's okay to reach out and touch someone. A pat on the back, a hand on the shoulder, a squeeze on the arm: all these gestures can be warm and meaningful expressions of affection without any sexual overtones.

David and Jonathan even kissed when they had to say goodbye (which was totally socially acceptable for men in their culture). In many cultures around the world, that's a manly thing to do. While we do need to exercise wisdom and discernment in situations where a touch can be misinterpreted or inappropriate, I also believe that a big ol' bear hug usually is just fine. True, there are some heartbreaking reasons why touch may never be comfortable for some of us, but let's not just dismiss it out of hand.

Two | Develop Regular Rhythms.

"Not neglecting to meet together, as is the habit of some,
but encouraging one another, and all the more
as you see the Day drawing near."

(Hebrews 10:25)

It's easy to maintain friendships with guys we see all the time. Maybe it's a neighbor or a co-worker or a fellow ministry team member. We cross paths without a whole lot of extra effort, so it seems like we're keeping in communication pretty well. But even so it takes some planning and intentionality to meet for the man-to-man, soul-on-soul kind of interaction that defines the depth of brotherly love we need and crave. Busyness and sometimes-excessive demands on our time make regular, meaningful interaction with a brother an elusive thing.

So get out your calendars and set some dates. Meet for breakfast every Thursday morning. Do lunch every other Wednesday. Play golf on the first and third Saturday of each month. Pray together every Tuesday evening. Figure out what works for both you and the other guy and go for it. Just as in marriage, sometimes we have to make appointments to spend time with each other. Sad, but true.

Three | Deepen Your Conversations.

"So, being affectionately desirous of you, we were ready to share with you not only the gospel of God but also our own selves, because you had become very dear to us."

(1 Thessalonians 2:8)

Heart-to-heart conversation, when we share opinions, seek advice, offer insight, describe a challenge, or vent about a frustration—these are what we need, men. Sure, lighthearted camaraderie is half the fun, but we shouldn't be afraid to go deep, to be transparent and vulnerable with a friend who we can trust with our confidences. It can be scary, yes, but oh so worth it. And of course, it's a two-way street: often it's the other guy who needs to unload. So then it's our turn to be that trusted, confidence-keeping brother in the Lord who simply listens and understands.

Christ is our example in this endeavor, of course, as he is in everything. Fully God and fully human, he is the epitome of manhood and the model of the type of friend we want to be and have. Right there with us, every moment of every day: "What a friend we have in Jesus!"

Reflection & Mentorship

Begin

- Bromance might be an allusion to brotherly love.

Unpack

- Are men scared of bromance? If so, why?
- What about brotherly love is good?

Inform

- Referencing Romans 12:10 above, how is giving honor to other men an aid in brotherhood?
- What are examples of brotherly affection?

Land

- List a few of activities you need to do for your Christian brothers.

Do

- Take action today.

Reconciling Friendships

It is only the great hearted who can be true friends. The mean and cowardly can never know what true friendship means.

CHARLES KINGSLEY

You're getting along just fine with your brother when suddenly you find that you don't see eye-to-eye on something. And the disagreement escalates a little, then a little more, until your friendship sort of devolves into hurt and frustration. It happens. There are at least as many ways for friends to fall out as there are friendships. But our God is a God of peace, and he would have us work toward restoring harmony when conflicts arise with people in our lives.

The book of Philemon is a story about just that potential for renewal. It's an account of reconciliation between Onesimus (whose name means "useful") to Philemon, a wealthy donor to Paul and leader in the early church. Onesimus was a runaway slave who Paul met in Rome and led to Christ before discovering that he knew Onesimus' owner, Philemon. Paul then sends Onesimus back to Philemon carrying a letter encouraging reconciliation between the two men. There is much we can take away from Paul's godly perspective of this age-old issue: rifts in relationships.

One | You Must Go Back to Go Forward.

"I am sending him back to you, sending my very heart."

(Philemon 12)

All of our relationships have context and history; we need to remember that matters. Paul reminds Philemon that Onesimus is a person of intrinsic value (he matters to Paul, just as he matters to God). Indeed, every person is important to God; his entire eternal plan was forged to bring his lost and loved people back into relationship with himself. Jesus is the proof incarnate that "God so loved the world." Even the most off-course, seemingly hopeless cases (yes, even the criminal hanging on a neighboring cross as Jesus was crucified) he rejoices to save. We have to see the bigger picture, to view people with God's eyes, not our own, and sometimes that is *hard* to do. But praise God, he helps us do it.

Two | Spiritual Renewal Changes People and Their Relationships.

"For this perhaps is why he was parted from you for a while, that you might have him back forever, no longer as a bondservant but more than a bondservant, as a beloved brother – especially to me, but how much more to you, both in the flesh and in the Lord."

(Philemon 15-16)

Onesimus had been Philemon's slave, but Paul was not playing bounty hunter here. His goal was not to return a slave to the owner. Instead, he hoped to encourage a transformational reconciliation, one in which the restored relationship between two men would reflect a brother-to-brother bond rather than their former slave-and-owner connection. So, if we are striving to see the people in our lives as God sees them, the nature of our interaction with them will inevitably be changed. Particularly if they are fellow believers, because then, scripture makes clear, we are bound together by virtue of our shared faith in Jesus Christ. They're family, so it behooves us to do everything we can to handle those relationships in a way that's pleasing to the Lord.

Three | Mediation & Bartering May Help.

"So if you consider me your partner, receive him as you would receive me. If he has wronged you at all, or owes you anything, charge that to my account."

(Philemon 17-18)

Paul was a friend to both men. He aimed to bring peace to their relationship. He took the initiative as a sort of mediator, and we can follow his lead by encouraging reconciliation between two feuding friends. But it also follows that if we ourselves are at odds with a brother we can and often should seek help from a cooler-headed third party, especially if that third party has some expertise in the art of conflict resolution. Be careful, though. Make sure your mediator can bring a spiritual viewpoint to the table and maintain a neutral perspective. It's tempting to engage a go-between who seems to side with you so that together you can present a united front. But that will only make your brother feel attacked, and distance him even more. Even if you sincerely believe your brother is behaving in a scripturally errant or un-Christlike way, you still want to identify a mediator who can help guide you through the reconciliation process in a thoughtful, sensitive, loving way.

Four | Be Willing to Make Amends.

"Confident of your obedience, I write to you, knowing that you will do even more than I say."

(Philemon 21)

To restore a relationship is—perhaps first and foremost—an act of obedience. We know that God is a God of reconciliation, so reconciliation is what we seek. But it does come at a cost. It requires that we set aside our ruffled feathers to see things from the other guy's point of view. It requires that we welcome each other, agreeing to learn whatever hard lessons are necessary. It requires that we correct any mistakes we've made and attempt to put things right. And it requires a decision to forgive, and a commitment to work toward restoring trust.

Our friendships are valuable. You know how it is when you've lost something that was important to you, or something you treasure gets broken, and how happy you feel when the lost is found or the broken repaired. Friendships are worth pursuing, and scripture encourages us to preserve those bonds: "If possible, so far as it depends on you, live peaceably with all" (Romans 12:18). After all, as brothers in Christ, we all end up together in heaven, forever!

Reflection & Mentorship

Begin

- Reconciliation is vital to all friendships. We should embrace the process.

Unpack

- Why is reconciliation hard for men?
- What obstacle prevents you from embracing reconciliation?

Inform

- In the process above, Onesimus was greatly challenged. What would have been challenging about reconciliation for Onesimus?

- What would have bee challenging for Philemon?
- What was challenging for Paul?

Land

- What challenges do you need to embrace?
- What steps do you need to take?

Do

- Reconcile with someone this week and share what you learned with a friend or a mentor.